INSTANT RAW SENSATIONS

By Frédéric Patenaude

About This Book

We are not responsible for the extreme fun you will have using this book and the wild food parties that might result. This book is intended purely as an academic, well-researched, scientific recipe book, and any pleasure you may get out of it is purely accidental. Please consult your doctor before attempting to have any fun.

Cover Art: Martin Mailloux.

All recipes by Frédéric Patenaude unless otherwise noted.

First Edition, June 2005
Printed in Canada on 100% recycled paper.
ISBN: 0-9730930-2-1

Published by:

Raw Vegan
6595 St-Hubert, CP 59053
Montreal (Quebec)
H2S 3P5, Canada
www.fredericpatenaude.com

Acknowledgments: First and foremost to Olivier, who's been pushing me for years to get this book done, to Adriane for helping me find the title, to Martin for his awesome cover, to Jay for his ideas, and to all the chefs, professional or not, who contributed to this book.

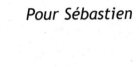

Pour Sébastien

Table of Contents

For Starters

If you are new to raw recipes, or you don't know exactly where to begin, here are my suggestions:

For a surprising smoothie, try the *Banana Mint* (page 14).

You need to try the *Fruit Soup and Wow!* (page 21), to give you an idea of how gourmet and satisfying a low-fat raw meal can be. Then you will want to try all the other fruit soup recipes.

A good green smoothie to start with is the *Banana Joe* (page 28), or the *Romans Gone Mad* (page 30).

For a raw soup, first try the *Roquette Me Soup* (page 38), or the *Indecent Gazpacho* (page 41). Also, the *Carrot Juice Soup* (page 44) immediately wins raving fans.

For a salad, first try my *Best Coleslaw Guaranteed* (page 56).

The *Best Non-Fat Mango Dressing* (page 59) is an experience you need to have soon (along with the *Delicious Non-Fat Salad* on page 51). The *Parsley-Strawberry Dressing* (page 59) will surprise you and your taste buds.

For a good dip, start with the *Cauliflower Hummus* (page 68)

For something imaginative, yet incredibly easy, make sure you try the *Take-No-Prisoners Submarine Rolls* (page 73).

For an easy and filling dessert, try the *Wow Coconut Cake* (page 81).

And of course, explore *2-Ingredient Recipes* (page 87) in the near future. It's definitely worth your time.

To be fair to my guest chefs (from page 96), I'll let you explore that section on your own.

Fred's Favorites

If I had to choose from all the recipes in this book (tough choice!), I would say the following are my favorites:

I am energized by the *Easiest Banana-Berry Shake* (page 17).

I could probably eat the *Absolute Mango Soup* (page 21) every day of the summer.

The *Basic Winter Green Smoothie* (page 27) is a staple, along with *Strange Brew* (page 28) and *Romans Gone Mad* (page 30).

In the summer, I live for *Indecent Gazpacho* (page 41). During the winter, I usually fall for something like the *Spinach-Arugula Cream* (page 46).

My *Still The Best Salad* (page 52) is still the best, although it's a tough choice, given all of the other recipes I reveal in this book.

For a dressing, I like the *Best Tahini Dressing* (page 60) or the *Avocado Mayonnaise* (page 62).

I rarely make dips, but when I do, I like the *Cauliflower Hummus* (page 68) or the *Easy Spinach Dip* (page 66).

The *Take-No-Prisoners Submarine Rolls* (page 73) also have my complete approval.

Above all, my favorite recipes are found in the *2-Ingredient* section (page 87).

Smoothies and Shakes Revisited

Smoothies are definitely one of the most basic and essential raw meals. For one thing, they are easy to prepare and to consume. One big smoothie can pack in enough fruit nutrition to give you energy for several hours or more. They are excellent for active people who need to consume extra calories.

When making smoothies, you may use water, but try to use as little as possible, so that you don't dilute fruit flavors. The high-water-content fruits are blended first, and the harder ones are added progressively. In my smoothies, I essentially avoid fat/fruit combinations, as these don't digest very well.

A quality blender, such as the Vita-Mix, is a good long-term investment and probably the best acquisition for the kitchen. For starters, any blender will do the job.

Enjoy these smoothies and shakes. May they inspire you to come up with your own favorite recipes!

Sweet Emancipation

Makes 2 servings

2 mangoes
2 cups freshly-squeezed orange juice
8-10 medium-size dates (or 4-6 Medjool dates)

Instructions:
Blend all ingredients together and serve.

Notes:
The sweetness of the dates cuts through the acidity of the orange juice and the mangoes. The result: a very enjoyable smoothie that will set you free.

Yellow Mint

Makes 1 large serving

2 mangoes
1 slice pineapple (1 inch thick)
1 small handful fresh mint leaves

Instructions:
Blend all ingredients together. Serve in a bowl or tall glass and decorate with a mint leaf.

Notes:
This is a refreshing and sustaining smoothie for the summer or spring.

Banana Mint

Makes 2 servings

3 large or medium bananas
1 cup water
1 small handful fresh mint leaves

Instructions:
Blend all ingredients together and serve.

Notes:
This is a surprisingly good smoothie that everybody will enjoy!

Basic Autumn Smoothie

Makes 1-2 servings

2-3 ripe persimmons
2-3 bananas

Instructions:
First, blend persimmons together. Add bananas progressively. Use water if necessary.

Notes:
A thick, sustaining smoothie that you'll want to make often during persimmon season!

Shelton's Refreshment

Makes 2 servings

4 cups watermelon
2 oranges

Instructions:
Blend all ingredients together and serve in tall glasses on a hot day. Use cold ingredients.

Notes:
Don't worry about the "wrong" food combining. Some people say we shouldn't mix watermelon with other fruits. It isn't true. They combine perfectly well, and they taste good mixed together!

Linda's Passion Pudding
By Linda

Makes 1 serving

1 mango
1 peach
1 pear

Ingredients:
Dice all of the ingredients and blend them slowly with an electric or hand blender.

Notes:
This makes a good pudding-like consistency and is sooooo good!

Red Snowflakes

By Mary Ziolo

Makes 1 serving

1 banana
Juice from 1/2 lime
12-15 cranberries
3/4 to 1 cup water*

* Depending on desired thickness.

Instructions;
Blend all ingredients and be delighted with the red snowflake effect.

Notes:
Mary: "This one reminds me of being a little girl, when I would shake one of those 'winter scenes in a glass ball,' and the snowflakes came falling down!"

Orange Wow!

Makes 2 servings

 3 cups honeydew melon
2 oranges

Instructions:
Blend all ingredients together and wow!

Notes:
Again, against the general rule of food combining, melons mix well with other juicy fruits. You can use any other white-fleshed melon for this recipe, but not cantaloupe.

A Surprising Nut Milk

Makes 2 servings

1/2 cups almonds*
1 1/3 cups water
5-6 dates
1 small apple

* Soak the almonds several hours in advance, if possible.

Instructions:
Blend all of the ingredients together. Strain through a cheesecloth or strainer.

Easiest Banana-Berry Shake

Makes 1 or 2 servings

4 bananas
1 cup water
1/2 cup raspberries

Instructions:
Blend the bananas and water first, then add the raspberries and finish blending.

Notes:
This is one of the best smoothies. I use just enough raspberries to give this banana smoothie a special touch. During the winter, you can use frozen raspberries.

Raw Popcycle Smoothie
By Rosanna Lalli

Makes 3-5 servings

3 cups freshly-squeezed orange juice
2 cups strawberries
1 large banana
1 mango
2 cups pineapple
2 cups crushed ice

Instructions:
First, chill your large shake glasses in the freezer while you prepare the fruit. Then, process all ingredients in a blender until smooth. Add the crushed ice after all of the fruit is blended. Remove your glasses from the freezer, which should be lightly frosted. Pour your fresh smoothie into your glass and enjoy.

Notes:
If a thicker smoothie is desired, cut back the amount of orange juice to 2 cups. If a thinner smoothie is desired, add more orange juice to taste. Any fruit in season could be used and substituted by taste. In the summer months, omit the crushed ice and pour into popcycle molds. You'll have fresh unsweetened popcycles that are good for you and your family.

Fruit Soups

In this section, I'll explore other ideas for fruit meals, beyond smoothies and salads. One of my favorite meals is a fruit soup. The fruit soup is simple to make. I use orange juice as the base for the soup, to which I add various fruits in season. I can also use blended mangoes or other blended fruits as the base. The following recipes will give you ideas on how to create new types of fruit meals.

Fruit Soup and Wow!

Makes 4 servings

This is one of my favorite dishes. I usually eat the whole thing by myself! Everybody loves it, especially children. There can be endless variations to it. Simply vary the fruits according to what's available and in season.

Winter Version

3 cups pineapple, diced
4 navel oranges, diced
4-6 kiwis, peeled and sliced
1 apple, diced
1 liter (1000 ml.) freshly squeezed orange juice

Instructions:
Mix all the fruit together in a bowl and cover with freshly squeezed orange juice. Serve in individual bowls.

Notes:
The quantities of orange juice may vary.

Summer Version

3 cups pineapple
4 peaches, sliced
1 cup strawberries, sliced
1 cup fresh raspberries
5-7 ripe apricots, or 1-2 mangoes, diced
1 liter (1000 ml.) freshly-squeezed orange juice*

* Or 1 liter of blended grapes (see page 101), or 1 liter of mangoes blended with a little water.

Instructions: See above.

Absolute Mango Soup

Makes 2 servings

This is an amazing dish that will blow everyone away!

2 cups freshly-squeezed orange juice
2 cups mango flesh
2 cups mango, diced

Instructions:
Blend the orange juice with 2 cups of mango flesh. Pour mixture into individual bowls and add in 1 cup of diced mangoes per bowl. If desired, decorate with slices of lime.

Summer Berry Soup

Makes 4 servings

1 liter (1000 ml.) freshly squeezed orange juice
2 cups fresh raspberries
1 cup fresh blackberries
1 cup fresh blueberries or strawberries

Instructions:
Mix all ingredients together. Let it sit for some time to let the flavors mix.

Notes:
This is a great soup to enjoy as often as possible during the berry season. I serve it as an entree before the dinner meal.

Gourmet Strawberry Soup

Makes 2 servings

4 cups whole strawberries
1/2 cup pine nuts or macadamia nuts
1 cup strawberries, sliced

Instructions:
Blend the 4 cups of whole strawberries until turned into
a liquid. Add in the nuts and blend until smooth. Serve
in individual bowls. Before serving, add 1/2 cup of
sliced strawberries to each bowl.

Notes:
Another fruit delight for the summer months. It can also
be used as a dressing!

Green Smoothies

The greener, the better...

Green smoothies are variations on the basic fruit smoothies. They explore the possibilities of combining fruits with green leafy vegetables. This combination digests surprisingly well and is one of the most satisfying and delicious of all.

The advantage of green smoothies is that they increase our consumption of green vegetables. You get the sweetness from fruit to give you energy, along with fiber and alkalinity from green vegetables. The result: an enjoyable instant meal that will take you to new heights...

The Basic Winter Green Smoothie

Makes 2 servings

1 apple
1 pear
2 bananas
1 1/2 cups kale
1 stalk celery
Water

Instructions:
Dice the fruit or cut in big chunks. Blend all ingredients together with about half a cup (up to one full cup) of water.

Notes:
You can vary the greens that you use for this recipe. Other good greens to use are spinach and lettuce.

Almost Tutti Frutti

Makes 2 servings

1 frozen or fresh banana
2-3 mangoes*
1 stalk celery
1 handful parsley
Water

* If mangoes are not available, use peaches, persimmons, or another type of sweet fruit.

Instructions:
Blend all ingredients together with about half a cup of water. Use more water if needed.

Banana Joe

Makes 2 servings

2 bananas
1 cup water
2 cups mixed baby greens*

* "Mixed baby greens" is a mix of various young greens. It can be found in most produce stores and health food stores. The best types are the organic brands.

Instructions:
Blend all ingredients together. Prepare to be super-charged!

Strange Brew

Makes 1 large serving

2 cups seedless grapes
2 cups mixed baby greens*

* "Mixed baby greens" is a mix of various young greens. It can be found in most produce stores and health food stores. The best types are the organic brands.

Instructions:
Remove stems from grapes and blend until the mixture is turned into a liquid. Add in the greens progressively and blend until smooth.

Spicy Mango

Makes 2 large servings

2 medium mangoes, diced
1/2 to 1 cup water
1/2 cup arugula
1 cup spinach

Instructions:
Blend all ingredients together, using more or less water as needed.

Notes:
The arugula gives a kick to this smoothie!

A Winning Green Smoothie

Makes 2 servings

2 cups papaya, diced
5-6 medium dates (or 2-3 Medjool dates)
2 frozen bananas
1 handful parsley
Water, as needed

Instructions:
Blend all ingredients together. Use a little water if needed to achieve the desired consistency.

Turn Me Sunflower

Makes 2 servings

2 mangoes
1 cup frozen or fresh strawberries
1 cup pineapple
1 big handful sunflower greens*

* Sunflower greens are known to sprouting enthusiasts.
They come from sprouting sunflower seeds on trays,
until the plant grows into a beautiful 6-10 inch green
vegetable. They are sold in many health food stores.
You can also grow them yourself at home. For more
information, check out books on sprouting.

Instructions:
Blend all fruit together, then gradually add 1 or 2 cups
of sunflower greens at the end.

Notes:
Organic frozen strawberries can be purchased in most
health food stores.

Romans Gone Mad

Makes 2 servings

4 bananas
1 to 1 1/2 cups water
2 cups romaine lettuce

Instructions:
Blend bananas and water together. Add romaine lettuce
progressively. Use more water if needed.

Pure Drive

Makes 2 servings

4 peaches
1 mango (or 1 banana)
2-3 celery stalks

Instructions:
Blend peaches until turned liquid. Add mango and then celery stalks progressively. Use some water if needed.

"Not Again, Mr. Green!"

Makes 2-3 servings

4 bananas
1 mango or peach
1 cup raspberries, frozen or fresh
1 apple
3 stalks celery
Water, as needed

Instructions:
Blend all fruit together, using water as needed for consistency. Add in celery stalks at the end, one at a time.

Notes:
Organic frozen raspberries can be purchased in most health food stores.

I'm Green, I'm Green

Makes 1-2 servings

2 cups papaya*, diced
2 bananas
1 or 2 cups kale

* Peaches can replace papayas.

Instructions:
Blend the papaya first, and then add bananas and kale progressively. Use more or less kale to taste. Add water for blending, if necessary.

Mango With a Punch

Makes 1-2 servings

2 medium mangoes
2 apples
1 1/2 cups kale or spinach
Water, as needed

Instructions:
Blend mango and apples together with water, as necessary to achieve a smooth consistency. Add kale or spinach progressively. Use more water if necessary.

Kale Lover

Makes 2 servings

3 bananas
2 apples*
1 cup water
1 1/2 cups kale or mixed baby greens**

* Golden, or other sweet kind.
** "Mixed baby greens" is a mix of various young greens. It can be found in most produce stores and health food stores. The best types are the organic brands.

Instructions:
Blend bananas, apples and water. Add kale or mixed baby greens and continue blending until smooth.

Raw Vegetable Soups
To Make You Invincible

Another basic raw dish is the raw soup. A well-known example of a raw soup is the gazpacho, a Spanish cold soup made from tomatoes and various vegetables. In this book, you'll find two raw versions of the gazpacho (on pages 41 and 115).

The raw soups I present go beyond the gazpacho. They are easy to make yet incredibly nutritious, refreshing and tasty. They can be light and juicy or very dense, depending on the ingredients used.

Raw soups are not only good during the summer months, but can be enjoyed throughout the year. In the winter, simply use room temperature ingredients and serve in a warm ceramic bowl. You could also heat them up a little using a skillet.

For more information on the art of making raw soups, please consult my book, *Raw Soups, Salads & Smoothies*.

Raw Campbell's Soup

Makes 2 servings

2 cups tomatoes
2 sweet red bell peppers, diced
Juice from 2 limes
1/2 cup almonds*

* For best results, almonds should be soaked overnight or several hours in advance.

Instructions:
Blend all ingredients together. Add a pinch of sea salt if desired — but it is good as it is!

Notes:
This is a nice little soup that reminds me of canned Campbell's soup, in a gourmet, much-improved version. Serve as an entree with a salad as the main meal.

Roquette Me Soup

Makes 2 servings

1 cup water
2 cups arugula (roquette)
2/3 to 1 cup fresh basil
1 avocado
3 medium or large tomatoes, orange or yellow*

* I like to use orange tomatoes because of their low acidity. If not available, use regular tomatoes, but only the ripest ones you can find.

Instructions:
Blend all ingredients except for tomatoes. Add the tomatoes last and blend just enough to leave tomatoes chunks in.

Notes:
This is one of my favorite soups, and it can also be used as a dressing! It is good without salt. If a saltier taste is desired, blend in 2-3 stalks of celery.

Greened-Out Soup

Makes 2 servings

1 cup cucumber
1 cup tomatoes
Juice from 1/2 to 1 lime
1 cup arugula (roquette)
3 stalks celery
1/3 cup dried tomatoes*
1/2 avocado
Dulse powder or sea salt to taste**

* Dried tomatoes should be soaked in advance, but if you use a Vita-Mix blender it is not necessary.
** Dulse powder can be found in most health food stores. If not, use your favorite seasonings. The soup is also good without anything else added to it.

Instructions:
First blend cucumber, tomatoes and lime juice until everything turns into a liquid. Then add the other ingredients progressively, and blend until smooth. Sprinkle with dulse powder or a little sea salt before serving, if desired.

Notes:
I like to use arugula in my soups and salads!

This Is What I Call Energy (Soup)

For Experienced Raw Eaters Only!

Makes 2 servings

The blended salad is a much thicker and heartier version of the raw soup. It contains more dark-leafy vegetables. Ann Wigmore used to call it the "energy soup." The sweetness of the fruit cuts through the bitterness of the greens. Here is one of my versions of it. Try it, and then vary it according to your taste. Remember, it is not necessary to use any fatty foods when making a blended salad.

1 cup mango, or another sweet fruit
Water (about 1/2 to 1 cup)
2 cups organic baby greens mix
1 cup lettuce, shredded
2-3 stalks celery, cut
1 small handful of dried tomatoes, soaked, or one fresh tomato (optional)
1 tsp. kelp, or a handful dulse (rinsed to take salt off)*
1/4 avocado, diced (optional)

* Powdered kelp can be found in most health food stores. You can also use whole leaf dulse (a seaweed), but rinse it off under warm water first, to take off the excess salt.

Instructions:
First blend mango or other fruit with water, then pro-gressively add all other ingredients. If desired, add chunks of avocado.

Indecent Gazpacho

A gazpacho so good you'll want to put your head in it and then rub it on your neck and chest!

Makes 3-4 servings

4 cups tomatoes
1 cup pineapple
2 cups cucumbers
1 garlic clove (optional)
1/2 tsp. sea salt (optional)
4 Tbs. apple cider vinegar, or lime juice
2/3 cup fresh dill or cilantro
2/3 cup fresh parsley
2 Tbs. maple syrup, or 2 dates

Instructions:
Blend all ingredients together. I personally use no salt and garlic, but if you enjoy that, you can add it in.

Add to the mixture before serving:

2 cups tomatoes, diced finely
2 cups cucumbers, diced finely

Notes:
You can let this gazpacho sit for some time in the fridge, to let the flavors mix.

Sexy Sweet and Sour Soup

By Janie

The true natural food gourmets will enjoy this.

Makes 1 serving

2 Tbs. tahini*
Lemon juice (to taste)
1-3 oranges or tangerines, peeled and seeded (either whole or halved sections)**
Chopped veggies of your choice (tomato, zucchini, celery and cucumber are good ones)
Baby spinach and/or lettuces or other greens (optional)
1 tsp. brown sesame seeds (optional)
Filtered water

* Tahini is a paste made from ground hulled sesame seeds. It can be found in all health food stores.
** You may substitute with cut pineapple as well.

Instructions:
Place tahini and 2 Tbs. lemon juice in bottom of soup bowl and stir until well blended. Gradually stir in more lemon juice until it is either soupy or sour enough for you (make it a tad more sour than you'd do if eating it straight). Stir in water until correct consistency and/or volume. Add oranges, tangerines or pineapple, veggies and greens to soup, stir and sprinkle with sesame seeds (optional) before serving.

Cauliflower Soup for Martians

by Karl Woods

Makes 2-3 servings

2 cups water
juice from 1/2 lemon (or to taste)
3/4 Tbs. sea salt
1 clove garlic
2 1/2 cups cauliflower florets, coarsely chopped
1/4 cup flax seeds, whole or ground
1 or 2 kale or collard
leaves, chopped (optional)

Instructions:
Place all ingredients in a blender and blend until smooth.

Notes:
Karl and his wife have been 100% raw for seven years. He wrote, "It has helped us to heal our bodies and awaken to the voice within."

Karl's website: www.FringeWisdom.com

Carrot Juice Soup

An all-time favorite!

Makes 2-3 servings

1 cup celery juice
2 cups carrot juice
1 cup carrot pulp
1/2 avocado
small handful dill, or cilantro
2 medium tomatoes, chopped
1 cup diced vegetables of your choice (cucumbers, peppers, etc.)
1/2 avocado, pieces (optional)

Instructions:
When juicing carrots, save 1 cup of carrot pulp. Blend carrot juice with avocado and herb (dill or cilantro). Add, without blending, the remaining ingredients.

Notes:
This soup will give you a reason to use that juicer you haven't used in months!

Instant Spinach Soup

Makes 1-2 servings

1 tomato
1 tsp. apple cider vinegar or lime juice
4 stalks celery
1 1/2 cups baby spinach

Instructions:
Blend tomato and cider vinegar (or lime juice) first.
Then add the celery progressively and finally, the baby spinach.

Variation:

Blend in 1/2 an avocado, and add one chopped tomato or cucumber to the soup before serving.

Notes:
This is an example at how simple and tasty raw foods can be!

Spinach Arugula Cream

Makes 2 servings

1 cup tomatoes
1 cup cucumber
1 lime (juice) or 2 Tbs. apple cider vinegar
1 cup arugula
2 cups spinach
3 stalks celery
1 small avocado
2 Tbs. dulse powder (optional)*

* Dulse powder can be found in most health food stores.

Instructions:
Blend tomatoes, cucumber and lime juice together. Add in the greens and avocado progressively and blend until smooth. Before serving, sprinkle with dulse powder if desired.

Notes:
Another great soup that could be used as a dressing!

Instant Veggie Soup

Makes 2 servings

2 cup tomatoes
2/3 cup pineapple
2 cups spinach
3 stalks celery or 1 cucumber

Instructions:
Blend tomatoes and pineapple first, add in other ingredients progressively and blend until smooth.

Notes:
You can vary this soup indefinitely by changing the vegetables used.

Some Great, Satisfying Salads

I probably make more smoothies and raw soups than salads. But it's also nice to make a beautiful salad of fresh vegetables in season. Short of simply eating your vegetables whole, making a satisfying salad is more than a great treat.

In my salads, I generally avoid mixing fruit with a fat, although sometimes I could mix an acid fruit with a fat. I use the salad ingredients that are in season. During the winter, I often add sprouts or sunflower greens.

Here are some salad ideas. For more information on the art of salad making, consult my book *Raw Soups, Salads & Smoothies*.

Delicious Non-Fat Salad

Serves 2-3

2-3 cups lettuce, shredded
2 cups arugula (roquette)
2 cups mung sprouts*
2 cups cherry tomatoes
Best Non-Fat Mango Dressing (page 59)

* Those are the sprouts used to make *chop suey*, available in most supermarkets.

Instructions:
Mix lettuce and arugula together. Add mung sprouts on top and decorate with cherry tomatoes. Serve with *Non-Fat Mango Dressing* to taste.

Dulse-Arugula Salad

Makes 2 servings

4 cups spinach
2 cup arugula (roquette)
2 cup whole dulse, rinsed*
Juice from 1 lime
1 avocado, diced

* Dulse is a seaweed that can be found in health food stores or ordered through the mail (www.seaveg.com).

Instructions:
Chop arugula and spinach. Add other ingredients, mix well and serve.

Still The Best Salad

Makes 2-3 servings

2 cups spinach
2 cups arugula
3-4 tomatoes (yellow or orange, if possible)
2 cups lettuce
2 handful dulse, rinsed (optional)*
Roquette Me Soup (page 38) or *Best Celery Dressing* (page 93)

* Dulse is a seaweed that can be found in health food stores or ordered through the mail (www.seaveg.com).

Instructions:
Mix all vegetable ingredients. As a dressing, use the *Roquette Me Soup, or Celery-Avocado Dressing*. If you want to use dulse, rinse it in water to get excess salt off, and then squeeze water out.

Orange Pecan Salad
By Becki Campbell

Serves 1

Green vegetables and lettuce
Oranges
Raw pecans

Ingredients:
Tear or cut up any greens you have on hand: spinach, chard, romaine, or leaf lettuce — enough for a large bowl. Dice segments from 2 oranges or tangerines (mineola or tangelos are the best!). Sprinkle with about 1/2 cup raw pecans. Slice another 2-3 oranges in half and squeeze over greens and pecans in bowl.

My Cute Little Bell Pepper Salad

Makes 2-3 servings

1 red bell pepper
1 orange bell pepper
1 yellow bell pepper
2 tomatoes, diced
1 cucumber, diced
1 cup fennel, chopped
1/2 cup sundried tomatoes, soaked*
1 avocado, diced
1/2 lemon, juice of

* The dried tomatoes need to be soaked in advance. If you're short on time, put them in hot water for 5 or 10 minutes.

Instructions:
Cut peppers either in cube or thin slices. Mix with other ingredients. Presentation is key for this recipe!

Mastodon Broccoli Salad
By Christian Mastor

Makes 2-3 servings

1-2 heads of broccoli *with stems*. . . (that's the best part!)
1-2 large handfuls of fresh basil, chopped coarsely*
1 red bell pepper, chopped
1 1/2 cups cherry tomatoes, halved
1/3 cup raw pumpkin seeds (soaked in water 10 minutes or not)
1-2 Tbs. diced red onion
1 avocado, diced
Juice from 1 lemon

* Don't be shy with the amount; I treat it like salad greens!

Instructions:
Cut the broccoli heads off the stems, leaving some stem on each flower.   Coarsely julienne the stems, and then cut in half (bite size pieces), but at an angle.   If the skin is too tough, peel it off.   Cut the flowers into bite sized pieces, lengthwise to maintain the flower/stem.   I prefer to leave all the broccoli pieces fairly robust and crunchy. Throw everything into a salad bowl, except tomatoes and half of the avocado. Toss until avocado breaks down just enough to coat everything. Add more lemon juice as needed.   Add the tomatoes and the remaining half of avocado at the end so they're not smashed.   Serve and enjoy!

Take-No-Prisoners Avocado-Spinach Salad

By Sadie DeSimone

Makes 2 servings

3 cups baby spinach leaves, washed and dried
1 avocado, diced
1 tomato, diced
4 thin slices red onion
Juice from 1 lemon
2 Tbs. pine nuts (optional)
Sea salt to taste, or your favorite seasoning (optional)

Instructions:
1. Place the baby spinach leaves in the bottom of a platter or salad bowl.
2. Lightly mix together the chopped avocado, tomatoes, and onions.
3. Place avocado mixture in a mound on top of the bed of spinach.
4. Mix together lemon juice and salt in a small bowl and pour over
salad.
6. Garnish with pine nuts, if desired.

Best Coleslaw Guaranteed

Avocado Mayonnaise (page 62)
Cabbage (red or green)

Instructions:
First, make the avocado mayonnaise (page 62). Double
or triple the recipe, according to your needs. Then, add
enough grated cabbage to create the coleslaw of your
dreams.

Notes:
If desired, add more lemon juice or apple cider vinegar
to give an additional punch.

Dressings You Never Thought Were Possible

A raw dressing doesn't need to be complicated. You don't even need to use oil in your dressings — I don't! The idea is to blend whole foods together, sometimes with something fatty, such as an avocado or some nut butter.

The following recipes will open your culinary horizons and inspire you to come up with your own variations!

Best Non-Fat Mango Dressing

Makes 3-5 servings

1 cup tomato
1 cup mango
2-3 Tbs. balsamic vinegar*
1/4 cup water

* Can also be replaced by lime or lemon juice, but it would be then a totally different dressing!

Instructions:
Blend all ingredients together and serve on any mixed salad.

Parsley-Strawberry Dressing

Makes 2-3 servings

I bet the naked chef wouldn't have thought of this one!

1/2 cup water
1 cup parsley
1/2 to 1 avocado*
1/2 cup strawberries

Instructions:
Blend all ingredients together. Add more or less avocado, depending on the consistency you want to achieve. Using 1 avocado will give a mayonnaise type of consistency, which is what I prefer. Use more water if necessary.

Best Tahini Dressing

Makes 2 servings

2 tomatoes
1 Tbs. balsamic or apple cider vinegar*
juice from 1/2 lime
4 Tbs. tahini.

* The balsamic vinegar can be replaced by more lime juice.

Instructions:
Blend all ingredients together and serve over a bed of greens. Mmm!!!

Tangy Curry-Mango Dressing

Makes 2 servings

1 cup mango*
1/2 cup water
1 tsp. curry powder
2-3 dates
2 Tbs. pine nuts

* You can use a mango that is not quite ripe.

Instructions:
Blend all ingredients together.

Notes:
Serve with tomato-cucumber salad (just tomatoes and cucumbers mixed together) — it's great!

Ultimate Dill Dressing
Makes 2 servings

1 cup cucumbers, peeled and diced
4 Tbs. pine nuts
3 medium dates
1 stalk celery
juice from 1/2 lemon
1/4 cup fresh dill

Instructions:
Blend all ingredients and serve on a bed of greens.
Remember to peel the cucumber first!

Notes:
You can serve this with a big salad. Start the meal with
fresh fruit and accompany the salad with another food
of your choice for a complete and easy meal.

Ridiculously-Good Ranch Dressing

1/2 cup tomatoes
juice from 1 lime
2 Tbs. apple cider vinegar (or juice of one more small
lime)
1/2 big red pepper, or 1 small one
1/3 cup fresh dill
1-2 stalks celery
4 Tbs. almond butter

Instructions:
Blend all ingredients together until smooth.
Notes:
The dressing is great without salt, but if you want a
more intense version, you can add some sea salt and
garlic. Try it unseasoned first.

Avocado Mayonnaise

1 tomato
1/2 lemon
1 handful basil leaves (fresh)
1 avocado
1-2 Tbs. kelp powder (optional)*

* Can be found in most health food stores.

Instructions:
Blend tomato with lemon juice and basil leaves. Add avocado and blend until smooth. Mayonnaise should be fairly thick. If desired, add kelp powder.

Notes:
This is a great mayonnaise. Use it to make an awesome coleslaw (page 56).

Dips, Pâtés & Side Dishes

When you want something substantial...

The following section presents various simple and delicious dips, pâtés and other side dishes. You can serve the dips with various raw or steamed vegetables, or use them as a dressing. So this section overlaps the dressing section.

With raw recipes, nothing is set in stone. A soup can become a dressing and a dressing can be turned easily into a soup. Likewise, a dip can easily be used as a dressing.

Avocado Dip or Dressing

Makes 2 servings

1 medium or large tomato
1 Tbs. balsamic vinegar*
1 Tbs. lime or lemon juice
1 avocado

* Can be replaced my 1 Tbs. lime or lemon juice.

Instructions:
Blend tomato with vinegar or lemon juice until liquid.
Add avocado progressively. Should be fairly thick.

Notes:
Serve as a dip with cauliflower and broccoli florets, or
steamed vegetables. Can also be used as a great dressing.

Easy Spinach Dip

Makes 2 servings

1 cup cucumbers
1/2 lemon, juice of
2 cups spinach
2 stalks celery
1 large avocado

Instructions:
Blend cucumbers with lemon juice. Add spinach and celery progressively. Blend with avocado until smooth.

Notes:
This is a great refreshing dip for the summer months. Can also be used as a dressing.

Veggie Pâté

Makes 2 servings

2 cups carrots, diced
4 Tbs. almond butter, or tahini
2 tsp. curry powder
Sea salt, to taste (optional)

Instructions:
Process all ingredients in a food processor. If a food processor is not available, grate the carrots instead, and mix with other ingredients.

Notes:
This pâté is quick and excellent. Everybody loves it!

Dulse Salad

Makes 2-3 servings

2 cups of rinsed dulse, chopped*
1 cup tomatoes, chopped small
juice from 1 lime
3-4 Tbs. tahini, or other type of nut butter

* Dulse is a seaweed that can be found in most health food stores (or ordered from www.seaveg.com)

Instructions:
Take two big handfuls of dulse, rinse in water to remove excess salt, and then squeeze water out. This should yield about 2 cups. Chop and mix in a bowl with other ingredients.

Notes:
Serve as a side dish with other green vegetables (such as mixed greens with *Best Non-Fat Mango Dressing* on page 59).

Cauliflower Hummus

Makes 2 servings

1 cup tomato, diced
juice from 1/2 lemon
2 cups cauliflower, chopped
4 Tbs. (or more) raw tahini
Sea salt (if desired, to taste)

Instructions:
First blend tomatoes and lemon juice. Add cauliflower progressively, then tahini. You should ideally use a food processor, if not a blender. I don't use sea salt, but you can add a little, if you wish.

Notes:
This is a great dip. Again, a great idea would be to mix this with mixed greens (such as baby green mix) and some tomatoes for a quick salad.

Raw & Spicy Pâté

8 Tbs. tahini
2 cups grated peeled parsnip or rutabaga*
1 1/2 cups grated carrot
2 garlic cloves (optional)
juice from 2 lemons

*Rutabaga is best.

Instructions:
Mix all ingredients in a food processor or blender to achieve a creamy consistency. Season with sea salt if you wish, but the recipe is great without it.

Notes:
Another easy pâté that will surprise you.

Let's Get Fancy (or Not)

More Raw Ideas

I couldn't call this section "gourmet raw cuisine" or anything like that. All the recipes in this book take 15 minutes or less to prepare! Their simplicity would horrify a gourmet chef, although you and I understand that Nature created the best gourmet foods — fruits and vegetables — which need very little processing to be turned into "gourmet delights."

So this section includes everything that's a little more imaginative and doesn't fit in the previous sections. Although I no longer want to make complicated recipes (the *Absolute Mango Soup* (page 21) is good enough for me!), I still like to impress with presentation, which is the key to making fun raw cuisine!

Take-No-Prisoners Submarine Rolls

Avocado mayonnaise (page 62)
Chopped broccoli florets
Mixed baby greens or baby spinach
Tomatoes or sundried tomatoes
Olives (optional)
Nori sheets

Instructions:
First, make a batch of *Avocado Mayonnaise* (page 62).
You can double or triple the recipes, if you're making
this for a lot of people. Then add several cups of
chopped broccoli florets — enough to keep it creamy
and tasty. Each "sub" will use several scoops of this
mixture that you'll spread on half a nori sheet. Add
greens, chopped tomatoes or sundried tomatoes (soaked
in advance), and olives if you desire. Roll up as you
would a sushi, and eat as a submarine!

Notes:
The variations on
this recipe are
obvious. For exam-
ple, you can
replace the nori
sheets with a
romaine lettuce
leaf.

Okra Popcorn
By LaMana Donadelle

15 pieces fresh okra
Olive oil*
Sea salt (to taste)
2 nori sheets torn into 1/2 inch pieces**

* Enough to toss okra.
** A seaweed that can be found in all health food stores and most supermarkets.

Instructions:
Mix all ingredients together in a bowl. Use just enough olive oil to toss everything together.

Notes:
Pop 'em in your mouth!

The Thai Plate

Serves 2

This is the dressing for two people:

1 cup freshly-squeezed orange juice
2/3 cups soaked almonds (1/2 cup when unsoaked)
1 tsp. curry powder
1/4 tsp. sea salt (optional)

Instructions:
Soak 1/2 cup of almonds to get about 2/3 cups soaked.
Blend all ingredients until smooth.

Salad ingredients, for each person:

2 zucchinis, shredded
1 tomato, cut
juice from 1/2 lime
Cilantro leaves, fresh
2 wedges of lime

Instructions:
You can shred the zucchini or slice it in more fancy
ways, using special kitchen tools if you have them.
Arrange all ingredients in a plate. The above ingredients
are for one plate (one person). Serve with dressing.

Presentation is key for this recipe! This is a very easy
dish to make.

Anti-Craving Veggie Wraps

By Miko Nelson

Serves 2 to 3

1 avocado
1 head cauliflower
1 chives (garlic chives are my favorite, but green onions will work)
Lettuce leaves

Instructions:
Take the avocado and cauliflower and chop like mad. Serve together in a bowl along with washed and cut whole chives and lettuce. Scoop mixture into lettuce leaves with chives. Season with sea salt and lime juice if desired — I like it unseasoned just fine. Wrap it up and chow down!

Notes:
Alternately, use nori sheets, instead of lettuce, to wrap.

It's Official: The Easiest and Tastiest Raw Sushi

I guarantee that these sushis will take minutes to prepare and will be as tasty as the best raw sushis you ever had. Are you ready?

For each sushi roll, you need:

1 nori sheet
1/2 cup of grated carrots
1/2 green onion, chopped
1/3 avocado, diced
1/2 teaspoon of curry powder (optional)
Thin slices of apples*
Sprouts (to garnish)
Optional seasoning: soy sauce

Instructions:
On half of your nori sheet, spread grated carrots, then add avocado in chunks, green onions, sprouts, apples. Top with curry powder and soy sauce (or tamari) to taste. Roll up, seal with some water, and cut up in pieces.

* For the apples, it's pretty simple. Cut a slice of an apple. Then I want you to cut little slices with them. You don't need much, but it really adds a punch.

Fred's Favorite Raw Burrito

Serves 2

You'll be impressed how tasty and easy this one is.

First prepare the burrito filling:

4 cups of tomatoes, diced small
1 avocado, mashed
2 tsp. curry powder
1 chopped green onion.
Sea salt or soy sauce to taste*

* You can also use dulse powder or flakes, or nothing.

Instructions:
Once you've prepared your filling, you'll take 1 *head of cabbage* and take the leaves apart. You'll use them as your burrito "bread". Simply scoop the burrito filling inside them and enjoy. You can do the same with big *romaine lettuce* leaves.

No-Compromise Desserts

With all these fruit recipes, if you're like me, you won't be craving desserts anytime soon. But hey, there are special occasions in life. And there are kids and family, too! For them, I have compiled a series of nice, no-compromise desserts. Of course, they are as easy as all the other recipes in this book.

Wow Coconut Cake

Makes 4 servings

In terms of satisfying and easy desserts, this one is hard to beat.

First, make the crust:

1/2 cup almonds
1/3 cup walnuts
5-7 dates
4 Tbs. dried coconut

Instructions:
Soak the almonds in advance for a few hours. You can soak the walnuts too. Then, in a food processor or blender, combine all ingredients together. Spread this mixture inside a Tupperware container or a pie container.

On top, add, in 3 different layers:

4 bananas, in big chunks or slices
4 Tbs. dried coconut
1 cup fresh blueberries

Instructions:
On top of crust, add bananas slices, dried coconuts, and finally blueberries. Serve immediately, or refrigerate to enjoy later!

Apple Cinnamon Jacks Cereal
By Erica Ayers

Makes 2 servings

1 orange
1/4 cup dried apples*, cut into small pieces
1/2 cup cashew pieces
2 tsp. agave nectar ** or other natural sweetener
1/4 tsp. cinnamon
Dash of nutmeg
1/2 banana (optional)

* Unsulfured and unsweetened.
** Can be found in most health food stores. Honey or another sweetener can also be used.

Instructions:
Squeeze orange juice with pulp into cereal bowl. Add agave, cinnamon and nutmeg and stir. Mix in cashews and apples. Top with slices of banana.

Raw Chocolate Turtles
By Tara

Bananas
Pecans
Cinnamon
Carob powder

Instructions:
Take ripe bananas and cut them into 3/4 inch pieces.
Then take a 1/2 of a pecan and press lightly into the
banana pieces.
Top with a dash of cinnamon and carob.   Finally, freeze
for one hour.

Notes:
Yummy frozen cold banana treats. They remind me of
those "chocolate turtles."

Sharrhan's Apple Fantasia

By Sharrhan Williamson

Makes 2 servings

2 small apples (preferably Macintosh)
1/2 cups dehydrated apple rings
2 handfuls raisins
2 Tbs. tahini
juice from 1/2 lemon
Cinnamon, to taste

Instructions:
Dice apples.   Cut apple rings into small pieces and soak in warm water for a couple minutes.   Put all ingredients in blender, adding a little water if needed. Process until well blended, but not completely homogenized.   (I blend in a food processor for about 30 seconds.)

Notes:
Makes a great dessert that is very satisfying.

Coconut Cake For Kids

By Adèle Arsenault

Unsweetned coconut flakes
Pureed dates*
Sliced bananas

* Can be made by blending pitted dates with a little water.

Instructions:
Mix a little water in the coconut flakes. Put enough of this mixture into a pie container, or other container you may have, to act as the crust. You can freeze this before continuing. Then add a row of pureed dates and a row of sliced bananas. Add some dried coconut flakes, and then a row of the moist coconut mixture, dates, and bananas. The last row will be dates. You can add some coconut flakes again to finish. Freeze for a few hours and thaw15-20 minutes before serving.

Notes:
This is a treat all kids love (and adults too!). The ingredients are easy to find. This makes a great birthday cake. In that case, simply add some candles.

2-Ingredient Recipes

More of the simple stuff everybody likes!

I thought this was too simple and obvious to put in the recipe section, but I also thought my readers should know about these recipes! They are the kinds that quickly become staples in your diet.

Sesame Cream

Makes 1 serving

1/3 cups whole sesame seeds
3-4 tomatoes

Instructions:
In a coffee grounder, process the sesame seeds. Then in a blender, blend tomatoes and then add in the sesame seeds. Blend until smooth. If you have a Vita-Mix, you can blend everything together without problems. You can also purchase pre-ground sesame seeds.

Notes:
Creates a cream that you can enjoy before your dinner or as a dressing. *For experienced raw eaters!*

Basic Banana Smoothie

Makes 2 servings

1 cup water
4-7 bananas

Instructions:
Blend water with bananas. Should be fairly thick.

Notes:
I often have this for lunch as a meal, often with more than 7 bananas!

Banana Water

Makes 2 servings

2 cups water
1-3 bananas

Instructions:
Blend bananas with water. Use more or less bananas to taste. Should be fairly thin — this is not really a smoothie!

Notes:
This is a great hydrating and uplifting drink. Athletes should definitely try it out.

The Best Ever

Makes 1 serving

Basic recipe:

2/3 cup mango
1/3 cup papaya

Instructions:
Just blend papayas and mangoes together for *the best smoothie ever*. The proportions are 2/3 mangoes and 1/3 papaya, so adjust according to your needs.

Apples With Snow

Makes 1 serving

2-3 sweet apples (golden, red delicious, etc.)
3-5 bananas

Instructions:
Peel and chop or slice apples. Mix in a bowl. Then, on a plate, mash the bananas with a fork. Add this on top of the apples. If desired, sprinkle with some cinnamon.

Notes:
Use sweet apples, not acidic varieties. This is a great meal that I eat several times a week during the winter. In fact, I double or triple this recipe.

Papaya Boat

Makes 2 "boats"

I eat 2-3 of these, and I'm satisfied!

1 large papaya
3-4 bananas

Instructions:
Take a large papaya and cut it in half. Scoop out the seeds and fill the hole with banana slices (about 1-2 bananas per "boat"). Eat with a spoon.

Notes:
The best papayas to use for this recipe are the big ones that come from Mexico or Central America.

Tomato-Tahini Dressing

Makes 2 servings

Tomatoes
Tahini

Instructions:
Blend a couple tomatoes until liquid. Add in a few tablespoons of tahini and blend until smooth.

Notes:
A quick and easy dressing! As a variation, blend in a few stalks of celery.

The Best Smoothie on the Planet

Makes 1 serving

Mangoes
Raspberries

Instructions:
The quantities are not important. Just know the ratio: 2/3 mangoes to 1/3 raspberry.

Notes:
All I can say is: aaaahhahhaahahaha!

Best Celery Dressing

Makes 2 servings

1 or 2 cups of celery juice
1/2 to 1 avocado

Instructions:
Blend celery juice with avocado. Use more or less avocado to taste. If you use more, it'll turn into a mayonnaise, which is also great! Serve with any salad.

Notes:
Okay, you need a juicer for this one. But maybe your juice bar can sell you some celery juice. In any case, it's worth to try it!

Soothing Cream

Makes 1 serving

Water
Apples
Celery

Instructions:
Blend apples with a little water. Add in many stalks of celery, to taste.

Notes:
This won't win any culinary award, but it may be just what you need once in a while. Try it, and you will be convinced.

Simply Delicious Fruit Meal

Makes 1 serving

1 papaya, diced*
2 bananas, sliced
1 orange

* Or 2 mangoes or peaches, diced or sliced.

Instructions:
Place in a beautiful bowl and squeeze a fresh and juicy orange over it all!

Tahin-Gin

Makes 4 servings

4 Tbs. tahini
4 big lettuce leaves

Instructions:
Spread 1 Tsp. of tahini on 1 leaf of lettuce and eat as a sandwich.

Notes:
4 of those make a nice meal (with a proper fruit entree).

The Best From The Chefs

Dave Klein

David Klein is publisher/editor of *Living Nutrition Magazine*, based in Sebastopol. David is also a Healthful Living Consultant, giving nutrition and self-healing consultations. David directs Colitis & Crohn's Health Recovery Services, and is author of *Self-Healing Colitis & Crohn's*.

Websites:
www.livingnutrition.com
www.colitis-crohns.com

BLT

6 large lettuce leaves
1/3 to 1/2 cup Brazil nuts, soaked, then ground
1 ounce sun-dried tomatoes, soaked
1/4 cup pine nuts, soaked
1 slice of a large tomato
Optional: 1 thin slice of sweet onion

Instructions:
Drain soaked sun-dried tomatoes, then blend with
ground nuts. Add water as needed to make a workable
mixture. Form the tomato-mixture into a patty.
Place the patty on 3 leaves of lettuce. Drain, rinse, and
blend pine nuts. Add water as needed to create a
creamy consistency. Spoon the pine nut mixture over
the patty. Optional: top with the onion. Top with the
tomato slice and 3 leaves of lettuce then enjoy!

Avocado-Dulse Salad

Approx. 1 cup of whole leaf dulse*
1 avocado, mashed
Optional: mint leaves

* Soaked then thoroughly rinsed.

Instructions:
In your hand, firmly squeeze the dulse to remove most
of the remaining water. Place the dulse in a bowl, and
then add the avocado. Garnish with mint leaves, if
desired, and top with your choice of veggies or cherry
tomatoes. Optional: blend fresh-squeezed lemon or lime
juice into the avocado. Blend together and enjoy!

Paul Nison

Raw-foods chef and educator Paul Nison has been eating a raw food diet since he was diagnosed with ulcerative colitis many years ago. With no other choice but surgery, according to the medical profession, Paul decided to stop eating all cooked foods. Today he is 100% cured of this so-called "incurable disease." Paul travels the world giving lectures on the raw life and food prep classes to show people how easy and fun the raw life can be.

Websites:
www.rawlife.com, www.therawworld.com

Mushroom Pizza

"When you just gotta have a pizza"

Portobello mushroom
Lemon juice
Tomato
Almond butter

Instructions, for each "pizza":
Take stem off mushroom, clean cap and turn upside down. That's the crust.

Pour the juice of one lemon over cap. Put about 2-4 tablespoons of creamy almond butter (could also use tahini or other nut butters and pâtés). Top with sliced tomatoes and enjoy.

Doug Graham

Dr. Graham is an advisor to world-class athletes and trainers from around the globe. He has trained professional and Olympic athletes from almost every sport, including tennis legend Martina Navratilova, NBA player Ronnie Grandison, and the Norwegian national bicycling team Dr. Graham is the best-selling author of *The 80-10-10 Diet*, *Nutrition and Athletic Performance*, *Prevention and Care of Athletic Injuries*, and several other books.

An inspiration to others, he has followed a raw-vegan regimen for over twenty-five years and has been vegetarian for over thirty years. He is living proof that eating whole, fresh, ripe, raw, organic food is the way to achieve vibrant health and vitality!

Websites:
www.foodnsport.com

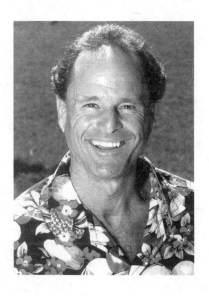

May the Best Mango Win

3 mangoes
1 pint raspberries, or 1-2 diced ripe bananas

Instructions:
Separate the cheeks from the pit of the mangoes and
scoop out the flesh. Dice the mango into bite-sized
pieces. Add one pint raspberries OR 1 or 2 diced ripe
bananas.

Great Grape Shake

Seedless grapes

Instructions:
Fill a blender with grapes. Blend and serve. (It is sup-
posed to be a little chewy, yes.)

Almost Instant Soup

Tomatoes
Celery

Instructions:
Remove leaves from celery and blend two celery stalks
for every tomato that goes into your blender. Leave this
soup slightly chunky for more chewing pleasure. Add any
ONE of the following ingredients will pleasantly and
completely change the taste and feel of this soup.

Cucumber, Bell pepper
Parsley, Citrus of any type
Pineapple, Kiwi
1/2 ounce of any nut or seed

Rozí

Professor Rozalind "Rozi" Graham, author of a book on health and fitness over forty, is widely recognized as a leading fitness and nutrition expert in England, where she teaches college-level nutrition courses. Rozi has trained many fitness and nutrition professionals throughout the U.K., and is a consultant for the Royal Navy. She works as a speaker, writer, and consultant on the topic of raw health creation, specializing in women's health issues, disordered, eating, and older adults. She is vice president of *Healthful Living International,* the world's premiere natural hygiene organization. Her articles are regularly published by numerous health, fitness, and nutrition magazines, including the Reader's Digest.

E-mail: healthyunlimited@aol.com

Berrimond

Mix **strawberries, raspberries** and **grapes** in a bowl.
Blend the juice of one **orange** with a few **almonds** until
smooth and then pour it over the top of the fruit mix.

Citrus Sunrise

Cut fresh segments of **oranges** and a **grapefruits** in half
and then mix them all together in a bowl. Blend
together some **strawberries** and **blueberries** and pour
the sauce over the top of the **citrus** chunks. .
Accompany with a glass of **freshly squeezed orange
juice,** then go and make your second helping!

Raspberry Refresher

This makes a great summer salad.

Chop and mix **tomatoes** and **cucumbers** - lots of each.
Cover with a blend of **raspberries, tahini** and **fresh
mint leaves** to taste.

Apples and Custard

Place two chopped **apples** in a bowl. Blend 3 ripe
bananas with 2 **dates**, a little water and a piece of
chopped **vanilla** pod, until really well blended.
Pour the banana custard over the top of the apples.

Cherie Soria

Cherie Soria is the founder and director of Living Light Culinary Arts Institute and the author of the classic *Angel Foods: Healthy Recipes for Heavenly Bodies*. She has been teaching vegetarian culinary arts for national and international organizations for more than 30 years and gourmet raw vegan cuisine since 1992. Cherie has personally trained many of the world's top raw food chefs and instructors and is often referred to as the mother of gourmet raw vegan cuisine.

Websites:
www.rawfoodchef.com
Phone:
707-964-2420

Garden Blend Soup

Yield: 4 cups (2 to 4 servings)

1 1/2 cups water
1/2 cup orange juice or 1 orange, coarsely chopped
1/2 bunch kale, stemmed and chopped (3 cups)
1 apple, cored and chopped
1/2 cup cilantro, fresh basil leaves, or fresh dill weed, packed
1/4 cup fresh parsley
2 tablespoons light, mellow miso
1/2 red jalapeño pepper, with seeds, or a pinch of cayenne
1 tablespoon lemon juice
1 clove garlic, crushed
1 green onion, optional
1 avocado, peeled and seeded

Instructions:
1. Combine water, orange juice, kale, apple, cilantro or other fresh herbs, parsley, miso, jalapeño, lemon juice, garlic, and the optional green onion, and blend until smooth.
2. Add avocado and blend again until smooth.
3. Serve immediately.

Notes:
The orange juice gives sweetness to the soup. For a less sweet soup, reduce or eliminate the orange juice, and replace it with additional water.

Variations:
You can use a variety of vegetables in garden soups, such as cucumber, zucchini, tomato, bell pepper, celery, romaine, and spinach.

Tim Trader &
Laurie Masters

Dr. Timothy Trader and Laurie Masters live in San Jose, California. Tim, a retired naturopathic physician with a doctorate in nutrition, serves health seekers worldwide through nutritional and lifestyle coaching and private supervised fasting. Laurie is a freelance editor, researcher, and writer. Together, they guide people to "stop fixing problems and start creating health." They teach a simple, low-fat raw diet in which fresh fruit takes center stage and tender greens are the sole supporting cast members (grains, legumes, supplements, dehydrates, juices, and oils play no role, and nuts/seeds make only rare guest appearances). Contact them at 800-242-0363, ext. 3803.

Peaches & Cream

This low-fat, well-combined dessert is a refreshing treat on a hot summer day.

Serves 4

4 large peaches, sliced
4 bananas
1/2 cup water

Instructions:
Blend bananas and water. Pour over sliced peaches. Serve immediately.

Chili

This is a low-fat, healthful alternative to traditional chili.

Serves 4, when combined with a simple salad.

3 cups tomatoes, diced small
2 cups red bell peppers, diced small
3/4 cup zucchini, chopped
1/4 cup sun-dried tomatoes (dry, not packed in oil)

Instructions:
Combine 2 cups of tomatoes and 1 cup of bell pepper with sun-dried tomatoes and zucchini in the blender. Blend well. Place remaining diced tomatoes and bell peppers into four serving bowls, then pour blended mixture on top. Serve immediately.

Optional: For a more authentic "chili" taste (though not recommended for optimal health), you may add 1/4-teaspoon cumin and 1/4 cup diced onion. Do yourself a favor and try the above recipe first... it just might surprise you!

Tonya Kay

Tonya Kay is a professional dancer, female athlete, and morbidly romantic life-loving artist. This gypsy has toured the world making music with STOMP, executing aerial stunt work with De La Guarda, and singing/dancing backup for Kenny Rogers. Once diagnosed and medicated as "biploar," Tonya Kay has experienced nothing short of miracles — now happy and medication-free and dispelling the myth that the raw lifestyle takes "work" by showing how effortless this is, even for a full-time traveler. It does not take a blender, dehydrator or even a kitchen — health is free and now!

Websites:
www.tonyakay.com

Cockroaches

Medjool dates
Raw hemp seed butter

Instructions:
Pit dates and fill with raw hemp seed butter.

Pre-show Flow

Bananas
Dinosaur kale (or black kale)

Instructions:
Wrap bananas in kale leaves and enjoy like a sandwich!

Storm and Jinjee Talifero

Storm and Jinjee form a raw family with their children Raven (10), Jome (7), Shale (3) and Adagio (5 months). Their web-based services offer Raw Food eBooks, Raw Pregnancy Information, The Anti-Aging Guide, Jinjee's Raw Journal, Raw DVD Magazines, our Daily Raw Inspiration email, The Raw Vegan Times online newspaper, and their Raw Food Documentary.

Websites:
www.TheGardenDiet.com

Raw Tabouli

"This is one of our staples that we eat all the time in different variations.
It takes about 10 minutes to prepare."

Quantities for the basic recipe:

1 bunch parsley
1 bunch cilantro
1 bunch green onions
1 cup cherry tomatoes
1 avocado

Chop the parsley, cilantro and green onions very fine, and dice the tomatoes and avocado. Mix in a bowl.

Mash up *another avocado* and stir in the juice of a *1/2 a lemon*. Spoon into bowl with the chopped stuff above, toss gently, and enjoy.

Optional: a pinch of *salt*, a dash of *oil*, a teaspoon of *honey*.
Optional: a handful or two of *almonds* (not soaked) in the blender and blend them up into a fine flour which you can add into the bowl (this is in place of cracked wheat).

Of course, you can add lots of different veggies for different versions of this treat.

Jay Iversen (Miracle Jay)

Miracle Jay loves making things happen and seeing people shine. He has been raw for over 13 years. Miracle Jay's favorite raw things are his vanilla bean slippers, and his favorite raw country is Brazil. Miracle Jay is committed to a life of pure love and sweet music.

E-mail: miraclejay@gmail.com

Figgily Wiggily for 2

10-18 large Calimyrna or Turkish figs
2 kumquats (or the juice from 1/2 small orange)
1/2 thumb fresh ginger root
Pinch of ground cinnamon

Instructions:
Soak figs overnight in water, slicing stems off in the morning. Place in blender with 1/2 cup of water. Add kumquats (or the juice of one half small orange). Add fresh ginger root, sliced. Add ground cinnamon (optional). Blend until a smooth, whipped texture is achieved, adding small measures of water if required. Pour this fertility sauce over morning fruit. Sprinkle with moist bee pollen.

Giselle Tarrés

Giselle's family owns ORGANIC, the largest, most happening vegetarian restaurant in Barcelona. ORGANIC is located in the arty Raval neighbourhood, at C. de la Junta Comerç 11, about a 4 minute walk from La Rambla. Giselle loves manifesting peak raw experiences.

Catalonian Gazpacho for 2

2 fat juicy ripe red tomatoes
1 big red bell pepper
1 big cucumber
Garlic or onion as desired
1/4 cup (or as desired) extra virgin olive oil
Juice from 2 full limes or 1 lemon
1 teaspoon cumin
Pinch cayenne pepper
1/2 teaspoon Celtic sea salt

Instructions:
Blend all ingredients until a course liquid texture is achieved. Serve in bowls, garnished with chopped chives and/or cilantro and pine nuts

Chad Sarno

Chad Sarno, certified chef, instructor and founder of Vital Creations, LLC Chef Services, is one of the most talented raw chefs at the moment. Chad has been traveling the globe assisting in recipe, menu and kitchen development in the opening of many restaurants and centers, such as Vitalities Kauai, world renowned gourmet restaurant, Roxanne's in San Francisco and one of Asia's top health spas, The Farm at San Benito. Amid this extensive travel, Chad provides in-home personal trainings, group workshops, catering events and restaurant consultation.

Website:
www.rawchef.org
Phone:
888-276-7170

Spring Consommé with Avocado, Chile and Baby Dill

Serves 4-6

3 cups cucumber water (6 cucumbers)
2 cups vine ripened tomato water (8-9 tomatoes)
2 tsp. high quality sea salt
1 cup coconut water (or filtered water)
1 clove garlic
1/4 tsp. fresh chile diced
2 Tbs. lemon juice
2 Tbs. flax oil
1/2 tsp. Cumin ground
2 Tbs. mint shredded fine
2 Tbs. dill feathers
1/2 cup avocado, diced (firm preferred)
1/4 cup vine ripened tomato, diced small
1/4 cup tart apple, diced small

Instructions:
To release the natural water from the cucumbers and tomatoes, place both into separate bowls. For the cucumbers, slice thin, sprinkle one teaspoon salt and massage the salt in, until the slices begin to soften and release water. For the tomatoes, chop, also sprinkle salt and massage them until their water is released. Strain off liquid with a fine mesh strainer, save the water for the broth and store the "pulp" for a future dish.

In high-speed blender, blend cucumber water and tomato water with coconut water, garlic, chili, lemon, flax oil and cumin. Pour again through a fine strainer to prevent foam.

In separate bowl, toss avocado, apple, diced tomato and mint together, place a generous amount of mixture in each bowl, pour soup over and garnish with a fresh dill. Serve chilled.

Nancy Desjardins

Nancy Desjardins, R.N.C.P., is a registered nutritional consultant practitioner. She works with her clients to improve organs and body functions, including the digestive system, circulation and hormones. She offers one-on-one counseling in the Georgetown, Ontario area.

Website:
www.healthlady.com
Phone:
905.873.0194

Hemp Seed Dressing

A classic sweet, creamy dressing.

- 1/2 cup hemp seed (shelled)
- 1/3 cup soaked raisin
- 1/3 cup fresh lemon juice
- 2 tsp. lemon zest
- 1 tsp. shredded or finely minced ginger
- 1 Tbs. Nama Shoyu (optional)*
- 1 clove raw garlic
- 1 tsp. cayenne
- 1/2 to 1 cup or more fresh water
- Celtic salt to taste

* Can also be replaced by tamari sauce.

Instructions:
In a blender, blend all ingredients until smooth. Store in a glass jar in the refrigerator

Rhio

Rhio, a leading proponent of the raw/living foods lifestyle, through her Raw Energy Telephone Hotline and website, provides information about health-related issues and raw and living foods events. Rhio is also the author of *Hooked on Raw*, a comprehensive 358-page book on the raw/live food lifestyle.

Websites:
www.rawfoodinfo.com, www.longevityradio.com

Beets in Orange Vinaigrette

Serves 4

3 cups grated beets
Juice from 3-4 oranges or tangerines
1 tsp. olive oil
1 tsp. thyme
Dash of Celtic sea salt and freshly ground white pepper

Instructions:
Mix all ingredients together in a bowl. Keeps for 3 days in the refrigerator.

Blueberry Jello

Makes 4 custard cups

1 pint blueberries
2 bananas
Juice from 1/2 lemon or lime

Instructions:
Blend all ingredients in a blender. Pour into custard cups and chill. Keeps for 2 days in the refrigerator.

Shazzie

Shazzie is the Managing Director of Rawcreation Ltd in the UK. She owns an online health store at www.detoxyourworld.com. She is author of *Detox Your World* and *Detox Delights*. Shazzie promotes raw foodism and natural health worldwide and has lectured in many countries. People love Shazzie for her ability to simplify the raw message, and her great British sense of humour! Her personal website, www.shazzie.com, has a huge following, with around 3,000 hits per day.

Websites:
www.shazzie.com, www.detoxyourworld.com

Medjool Mould

10 medjool dates, stoned
1 cup of sunflower seeds, soaked
Dried mango to decorate (or other dried fruit)
1/2 papaya

Instructions:
In a food processor, blend dates and seeds until you get
quite a smooth mixture. Pile it into little ramekin dishes
and put it in the fridge for about an hour. You should be
able to tap the moulds out onto plates by running round
the sides with a knife, turning upside down on a plate
and banging the bottom! Once it's turned out, cut really
thin strips of dried mango and lay on top in a criss-cross
pattern. Cut the papaya into little cubes and pile on
top. For a really special touch, add some edible flowers.

Jeremy Safron

Jeremy Safron began his studies in raw/living foods over 11 years ago. Teachers such as Dr. Ann Wigmore and Bernard Jenson contributed greatly to his education, although experience would turn out to be his most potent teacher of all. Jeremy has written 5 books and also composes music and designs software and food products. Jeremy has helped open 8 raw-food restaurants, including 2 of his own, and has educated thousands of people worldwide. He has been an avid student of yoga and martial arts for over 24 years and continues to practice and pursue transformational disciplines from all over the world.

Website:
www.lovingfoods.com

Amazing Apple Cobbler

This cobbler has continued to be a quick and easy, yet delicious recipe that was always was a big hit at the workshops.

Serves 4

4-6 apples, peeled*
5-8 soft dates
3 cups walnuts
1 Tbs. cinnamon
2 cups water
1 vanilla bean
1 orange
10 berries

* Pick the best ones you can get. Braeburn, Fuji, or granny smiths are my preferred varieties.

Instructions:
Pit dates and soak them in 1 cup of water. Split walnuts into 2 equal portions. Soak 1 & 1/2 cups of nuts in 1 cup of water. Either shred apples, or slice them into matchsticks by cutting thin slices off the side of the apple and then cutting those into thin strips. Squeeze the juice of the orange onto the apple strips.

In a blender or food processor, grind the dry portion of the walnuts into powder. In a bowl, mix up the apples, walnut powder, cinnamon and orange juice. Drain the soaking nuts and discard the water. Place the soaked dates and their water, the soaked nuts, and the inside of the vanilla bean in a blender or blender cup. Blend until creamy, adding more water if needed. Press the apple mixture into a bowl, so it has an even surface. Spread the nut cream mixture over the top of the apple mixture. Decorate with the berries.

Alex Malinsky

Alex Malinsky is an award-winning chef and has authored numerous articles, interviews, and newsletters on the raw and living foods lifestyle. At age 19, he is already a leading expert and has been on the 100% raw food lifestyle for over 6 years. He is a talented website designer and webmaster.

Website:
www.rawguru.com

Stuffed Avocado

Serves 1

1 ripe avocado
1 small ripe tomato, cut into 1/4-inch dice
1 tbs. fresh lemon juice
1 tsp. green onion
2 tsp. raw pumpkin seeds
1 tbs. fresh herbs (dill, parsley, basil, etc.)

Instructions:
Halve avocado lengthwise, and remove the pit. Top each half with tomato. Drizzle with lemon juice, and garnish with green onion and pumpkin seeds. Season with salt and enjoy!

Green Salad with Ginger Lime Dressing

Serves 6

3 tbs. olive oil
3 tbs. sesame oil
juice from 1 lime
1 1/2 tsp. honey
1 1/2 Tbs. peeled and grated fresh ginger
Sea salt to taste
1 head green leaf lettuce, torn into bite-size pieces
1/2 cup fresh curly-leaf parsley leaves
1 kiwi, peeled and thinly sliced

Instructions:
In a large bowl, whisk together olive and sesame oils, lime juice, honey, and ginger. Season with salt. Add lettuce and parsley. Toss to combine. Transfer to a serving platter, and garnish with kiwis.

David Norman

Real estate developer David Norman is the owner of New York's raw-food restaurant *Bonobo's*. Overlooking Madison Square Park, *Bonobo's* features the best and healthiest salad bar experience you'll ever have. Where else can you find raw fennel or celeriac in a salad bar? Bonobos has it all and more.

Bonobos share 98.4% of our genetic code and are the closest animal to humans. Those friendly creature also eat a diet of raw fruits and vegetables and would certainly feel more at home in David Norman's restaurant than in any other in North America.

Phone: (212) 505-1200
Address: *Bonobo's*, 18 East 23rd St. New York City
Website: www.bonobosrestaurant.com

Hazelnut Butternut Squash Soup

Makes about 18 oz, or 2-3 servings

1 cup butternut squash, shredded
1 1/2+ cup purified or distilled water
1/2 cup hazelnuts
Pinch Celtic sea salt
Favorite sweetener to taste (recommended: raw agave syrup or dates)

Instructions:
Blend hazelnuts with water and salt until creamy. Add shredded butternut squash and blend well until smooth, adding water if necessary to get hearty consistency. Add sweetener to taste. This soup should be a little on the sweet side. Serve with a few crushed hazelnuts on top.

Karen Knowler

Karen Knowler is head of The Fresh Network, Europe's largest raw food organization, based in the UK, editor of *Get Fresh!* magazine and co-author of *Feel-Good Food: A Guide to Intuitive Eating*. A popular writer and speaker, Karen regularly appears in the media, writes for national publications, appears regularly on television, and lectures internationally. She is currently working on her second book.

Website:
www.fresh-network.com

Dried Fruit Compote With Nut Milk

A delicious and filling breakfast that is perfect after a busy morning's work, or if you wake up ravenous. Simply spoon your chosen combination of soaked dried fruits into a large bowl and top with nut milk for a deliciously filling and satisfying breakfast.

Dried Fruit Compote

Instructions:
Begin by soaking a selection of **dried fruits** in pure water for a few hours, until they are nicely plumped up. You could do this overnight to save time in the morning.

Some dried fruits which work well are: Prunes, raisins, dates, apple rings, pears, peaches, apricots, figs. Any or all of these will work well together.

Nut & Seed Milks

Nut & seed milks are so easy to make and are wonderful on their own as a drink or snack, blended with banana for a creamy banana drink, or used as a pour over for a *raw muesli* or *fruit compote*.

Instructions:
To make a nut or seed milk, simply pour some pure **water** in a blender and add any **nut** or **seed** of your choice (best to use just one nut or seed at any given time). Next, blend the nuts/seeds and water together until a nice "milk" is formed. You may choose to strain the milk before serving. It's really that simple. You can make your milk as watery or as creamy as you like by changing the amount of nuts/seeds and/or water you put in.

Notes:

I recommend soaking all nuts or seeds before using to make them "alive," so it would be best to soak them overnight in a bowl of water (drain before using). This is not necessary, but it is easier on digestion, and soaked nuts and seeds often taste better.

Other good milks to try are: Cashew, sesame, sunflower, hemp, coconut. All are great sweetened up with some fresh or dried fruits, such as date and apricots, or add a little carob for a chocolaty flavor, or some vanilla.

Index of Recipes

Smoothies and Shakes Revisited

Fruit Soups

Green Smoothies

Raw Vegetable Soups

Some Great, Satisfying Salads

Dressings You Never Thought Were Possible

Dips, Pâtés & Side Dishes

Let's Get Fancy (or Not)

No-Compromise Desserts

2-Ingredient Recipes

The Best From The Chefs

Other Available Products by Frédéric Patenaude

500 PAGES OF INFORMATION AND INSPIRATION

To Order — Use Order Form

The **JEAA Compilation** is a reprint of the first 17 issues of the raw-food magazine *Just Eat An Apple* that were published in California by Nature's First Law and Frederic Patenaude. These magazines are now very rare.

The spiral-bound book features over 500 pages of information, articles, recipes, tips, questions and answers, testimonials, letters from the readers, resources, that you will not be able to find anywhere else.

It represents 5 years of work and thousands of hours of research. A unique compilation, printed in limited quantities.
A $102 value -- only $49.95.

IN THIS UNIQUE COMPILATION, YOU WILL DISCOVER:

* How to get warm during the winter on a raw-food diet.
* Why carrot juice is not as healthy as you have been led to believe.
• How to raise healthy cats and dogs on the raw-food diet.
* What are the symptoms of detoxification when we change our diet and what they mean.
* How an artist improved his art by going on a raw-food diet.
* Why mass media is mind pollution.
* The proof why organic food is better for us.
* How to slow down the aging process.
* The sexiest way to eat a mango!
* The truth about underwear (that no one told you!).

The Raw Secrets — The Raw Vegan Diet in the Real World —
2nd Edition, Completely revised and expanded.
By Frédéric Patenaude — $24.95

*This book is currently only available on the
Internet: www.therawsecrets.com*

The Raw Secrets will help you live sustainably on
the raw vegan diet and overcome the problems
you may have encountered in doing so.
Based on logical principles, the raw vegan diet
still often falls short of expectation. Instead of
improvements in their health, many people see
deterioration. Others experience less rejuvenation than they antici-
pated, or find themselves unable to maintain balance in the long-
term. This results solely from a lack of understanding of the guiding
principles of natural diet, from the widespread misinformation
about it, and the gross errors that follow. The 28, succinct chapters
give unique insights on many topics affecting those considering a
high-raw or all-raw diet. Each holds dozens of tips to help you eat a
pure, simple, nourishing diet.__ If you are tired of the same, bor-
ing, repetitive information found in nearly every other book on the
raw vegan diet, then you're in for a surprise!

If you seek groundbreaking research and a fresh perspective on raw
eating, you will find them in *The Raw Secrets* !

Raw Soups, Salads and Smoothies
By Frédéric Patenaude, $12.95 (Booklet)

Raw Soups, Salads and Smoothies contains delicious raw food recipes that are both tasty and
simple to prepare. In addition to the recipes, you
will also find useful and detailed information on
the art of preparing raw soups, salads and
smoothies, as well as a complete description of
some of the ingredients used in the book.
Contains over 60 easy and tasty, completely *RAW
soups, salads and smoothies recipes.*

**E-mail to Request a Complete Catalog of Our
Products:** catalog@fredericpatenaude.com
Or use the order form on the next page.

QUICK ORDER FORM

Online Orders: www.fredericpatenaude.com
Postal Orders: See below.
FAX: Please fax your order to: (514) 221-2177

Please send me:

___ copies of the book, *Instant Raw Sensations,* at $19.95 ($22.95 Canada) each.

___ copies of the *The Just Eat An Apple Compilation* at $49.95 ($59.95 Canada) each. (Please add an extra $10 shipping per book, due to its size. $20 outside North America.)

___ booklets, *Raw Soups, Salads & Smoothies,* at $12.95 ($14.95 (Canada) each.

___ copies of *Frederic Patenaude's Catalog,* FREE

SHIPPING: USA and Canada, please add $5 for one book, $3 for each additional book. Other countries, please add $9 shipping for one book, $6 for each additional book. Please apply shipping extras for *The Just Eat An Apple Compilation.*

Name: _____
Address: _____
City: _____ State/Province: _____
Postal Code: _____ Country: _____
Telephone: _____ E-mail: _____

Payment (in US Funds): ❐ Check ❐ Money Order ❐ Credit Card:
❐ Visa ❐ MasterCard
Card Number: _____
Name on card: _____ Exp. date: _____/_____

Send your order to:

Raw Vegan
6595 St-Hubert, CP 59053
Montreal (Quebec)
H2S 3P5, Canada

Comments:_____
_____
_____

*Now that you've bought
Instant Raw Sensations...*

Frederic has weekly, politically-incorrect, health & nutrition news for you!

Are you looking for:

- Exclusive interviews with top authorities
and unique thinkers in the field?
- Informative and thought-provoking articles?
- Useful advice and tips?
- The latest relevant research, not just the newest fad?

*You'll find all of that and more in the
Pure Health & Nutrition E-Zine*

All of this is absolutely free!

TO SUBSCRIBE TO MY WEEKLY E-NEWSLETTER

"PURE HEALTH AND NUTRITION"

Visit my website (click on "Newsletter"):

www.fredericpatenaude.com

About the Author

Frédéric used to stay up late at night, trying to figure out the exact proportions of water and banana needed to make the best banana smoothie he ever accidentally made — the one that tasted so good once, but that he's never been able to reproduce since. At some point, he gave up, and decided to just eat an apple.

Fred doesn't have spare time, but if he did, he would spend it eating more raw food and not getting fat.

Unless you go to his website immediately, you will never know who Frédéric Patenaude really is...

www.fredericpatenaude.com